Jesu
Then &

John Simmonds

St Marks CRC Press Sheffield

Together in Hope –
Resources for Christian Faith Today

This series of resource books is the result of a number of organisations working together to give encouragement and hope to those who seek a credible Christian faith for the twenty first century.

We hope that these books will be helpful to those individuals and groups, inside and outside the Church, who are exploring matters of faith and belief.

We are grateful to our authors and encourage others to offer their services.

For further information about the sponsoring organisations please see the back cover. If you wish to contact the editorial group,
email: **togetherinhope.editor@gmail.com**

The current convenor is Adrian Alker

A personal note

Jesus – Then and Now is the second of two publications which take a fresh look at the life of Jesus.

The first, **Walk the Jesus Walk**, invited people to examine the impact Jesus had on his first followers and to consider how they might engage with him today. Walk the Jesus Walk might be of special help to those who wish to explore the Christian way of living or to young people's groups in churches.

Jesus – Then and Now invites people to dig deeper into the Jesus story in the belief that the Good News which he proclaimed and embodied can be a potent force for good in the contemporary world.

Throughout my life I have tried to make sense of the Jesus story, first as a child in Sunday school, then as an eager young evangelical. By my mid-twenties, I was a Methodist minister, finding out that traditional Christianity raised more questions than it answered. So I committed myself to a new pilgrimage in theology. Throughout the journey, I was brought back to the story of the enigmatic Jesus of Nazareth.

In a busy life, I found insufficient time to read many large tomes, yet, from articles, reviews, talks and conversations, I gleaned much to get me thinking. Pictures, movies and documentaries also lent their wisdom. Moreover, there were enquirers to respond to, many who could no longer cope with traditional dogmas and interpretations. I, too, had lost sympathy with the great meta-narrative of Creation, Fall and Redemption as celebrated in Christian doctrine and liturgy. In particular, I could not relate to the Sovereign Redeemer figure that Jesus had become.

So I had to set to, and seek out the first Jesus. Was it possible to discover Jesus as he was before the church got its hands on him? It soon became clear that it would be difficult, even impossible, but one had to try.

Many people provided inspiration. Scholars, poets, artists, actors, movie makers - all contributed to my search. Above all, conversations with countless numbers of people in hundreds of settings have encouraged and informed me.

Because I owe so much to so many, I couldn't even begin to acknowledge which insight came from where. Sincere thanks and apologies to those who quickly discover that I have taken on board their ideas and represented them as if they were my own.

I have written this material because people say they are thirsty for exploratory material around the life and ministry of Jesus so that they might find in him an inspiration for contemporary living. So here's my contribution.

John Simmonds. January 2010

JESUS: Then and Now

This booklet is designed to help individuals and groups explore who Jesus was, who he became, and what it means for people to be his followers in this Third Millennium.

Whilst the sections can be used privately, it would be really helpful to discuss the material with other people. In a group setting, each session should provide ample opportunity for participants to share ideas and explore together.

It is unlikely that, by the end of these seven sessions, we will have settled every question about Jesus or what it means to follow him today. However, there is a good chance that we will have been touched by him and, hopefully, motivated by him.

JESUS: Then and Now

Contents

Introduction

When reading the four Gospels, people are soon aware of both their similarities and differences - not surprising when they were written by people in different church communities, at different times and with different presuppositions. Moreover, as they read, people inevitably interpret what they read in a variety of ways.

So remember that, whenever a gospel story is retold, it contains various elements:

- Some early impressions of the words and actions of Jesus.
- Ideas which come from the church as the gospels were translated, studied and expounded.
- The reader/teller's own emphases (personal and cultural).

It's clear that these various elements are involved and they always have been. Put them another way:

- The original events and earliest records.
- How the church handled the earliest records down the centuries.
- How I/we take up the story of Jesus in my/our personal experience.

These three areas are explored in the first five sessions.

Then in the last two, we will attempt to find:

- a contemporary way of talking about Jesus and
- a way of living which takes Jesus fully into account.

1 Who was Jesus?
Looking at the earliest records

The earliest followers of Jesus did not leave written accounts of his life. We have no diaries, letters, inscriptions, pictures, photographs or newsreels.

The earliest written references come in Paul's letters. These refer to

- his descent from David (Romans 1: 3)
- being buried and rising again, appearing to Cephas (Peter), then to the twelve apostles and later to five hundred people (1 Corinthians 15: 3-6)
- the institution of the Last Supper (I Corinthians 11: 23-25)
- a reference to James, the Lord's brother (Galatians 1: 19)

The Gospels

These were written by second, even third generation believers. Though each one is committed to Jesus and his Way, none tells the whole story and each tells the story in his/her own way.

There are a few mentions of Jesus in early secular writings, but little more than that he was crucified and had followers.

Also there are other 'gospels', such as those under the names of Thomas and the Hebrews, but these were not accepted as authentic when the church shaped up the Christian Bible late in the 4th century.

Three of the gospels, the Synoptics, are rather alike: they are Matthew, Mark and Luke.

Mark, written around 65CE, is written in an eager style and is somewhat unpolished. It may well have been written at a time of persecution and emphasizes the cost of discipleship.

Mark portrays a Jesus who

- was given God's spirit at baptism;
- obeyed God in such a way that he was called 'Son of God';
- announced the dawning of a new age;
- challenged people to change their ways and live for God.

Mark believed Jesus was the Christ - God's promised Messiah. He gives us a very human picture. Though filled with the Spirit of God, Jesus is not a God. His sonship is about relationship and obedience, not status.

Matthew, writing around 80CE, seems to come from an early Jewish / Christian setting. Although he bases his gospel on Mark's gospel, Matthew develops the story in his own way, possibly to be used liturgically i.e. to be read in sections throughout the year.

Matthew believes that Jesus is a new Moses, bringing a new law and leading people out of slavery. Hence Jesus is the one who fulfils the Old Testament promise of the coming of a Messiah who will save his people and establish God's kingdom, not just in Israel but throughout the world.

The disciples are Jesus' chief agents in this mission to the world.

Luke, writing around 85CE, seems also to have written in a Jewish/Christian setting, possibly in a Gentile city. He also bases his gospel on Mark and probably knew Matthew's work. He emphasizes that Jesus embraces everyone: foreigners, sick people, religious outcasts, women, children and especially the poor. People will come from east, west, north and south to sit at the feast in God's Kingdom. Jesus is not only the Messiah of Israel, but is also God's gift to the world. Perhaps Luke's interest is autobiographical; maybe he is an outsider trying to get in!

These three gospels agree in general that Jesus is

- a spirit-filled Jewish man, whose actions show the love of God,
- a mystic, with an intimate relationship with God, whom he called 'Abba' (Father),
- a prophet, speaking authentically about God and for God,
- a Messiah, God's agent bringing in the final days and calling people to change their ways and make ready for God's new world,
- God's vindicated one, his son, whose life stands in spite of death.

John's gospel was written much later (around 100CE) independently of the others. It seems to be related to the Epistles of John and was probably written for a separatist movement, under threat by Jews. The urgency of the Synoptics has gone. No longer is the return of Christ imminent. Moreover, the memory of the historical Jesus, such as it was, is fading.

In John, people's experience of God is much more individualistic. Jesus is portrayed as an eternal figure, though not yet the third person of the Trinity, but much more God-like in his attributes:

- In John chapter 1, Jesus is described as the Word (of God), who existed at the beginning of time, through whom the world was made.

- In John chapter 17, he is described as being 'one with the Father' and yet he is an obedient son.

So we have 4 portraits of Jesus....

- each one shaped by the authors,
- using bits and pieces of tradition, both spoken and written,
- with stories from their own community,
- incorporating convictions from the Jewish faith,
- and each in their turn shaped by their environment.

So how do we handle all this?

It's important to realise that we, in our turn, will impose patterns of our own upon the gospel material. We will tend to ignore difficult and uncongenial parts of the story and emphasise parts which fit our view of the world. For example, how often have you heard read in church the story of the coin in the fish's mouth (Matthew 17: 24-27) ?

So what does all this say about the way one reads the Bible?

One could say that the Bible is a human book, written by people who were trying to make sense of life, using many kinds of medium in their attempt.

The Gospels are the products of people who had the conviction that they had seen God's will for the world most fully expressed in Jesus of Nazareth. They expressed this in a variety of ways according to their own personal and communal experience. We simply don't know whether they got everything right. Just as we may argue with contemporary Christians, so it seems right to argue with the gospel writers!

This is what Sydney Carter, poet and song-writer, had to say about the way in which the Christian story evolves:

For forcing us to exercise faith on a heroic scale, Christianity could hardly be improved on. By Christianity I mean the whole perplexing, exasperating, mind blowing apparatus by which the messages of Jesus have been handed down. It dangles before us, not a saving certainty, but a bright, blurred possibility that fills the heart with hope and discontent and dares us to make the necessary leap. Christianity kindles the imagination; through all the broken and corrupted variants we catch the echo of the song behind the song. Does it come to us from the past or from the future? We can never know. The Gospels, the written records, play their part; but they cannot give us the kind of certainty we look for. Christianity is incurably folk: it forces us to recreate it. If we cannot, it will die. ('Rock of Doubt': A.R. Mowbray 1978)

Having said all this, what can we say with reasonable certainty about Jesus of Nazareth?

1. He came from Nazareth in Galilee and was the son of a carpenter, and possibly a carpenter himself.

2. He was a follower of John the Baptist, a revivalist preacher, who called people to return to a true way of living and be baptised. Jesus clearly had a great deal of sympathy for what John had to say.

3. Jesus believed that he had a special vocation:
   - this came from his intimate relationship to God, whom he called 'Abba' – 'daddy';
   - his vocation was to bring Good News to the poor and to people who were normally excluded from Jewish society and religion;
   - his healings and exorcisms were signs of the dawning of a New Age (the 'Kingdom of God' or the 'Kingdom of Heaven').

4. Jesus may well have called himself Son of Man (a name dropped by the early church). His followers called him

Messiah (Christ). Both names (Son of Man and Messiah) were names used in the Old Testament to describe the person sent by God to bring in a new age.

5. He gathered disciples, some of whom were social outcasts. He welcomed 'sinners' - the 'unclean' and 'outcasts' - into the Kingdom of God. Hence he drew round him a popular movement.

6. He taught in a way which came into conflict with established religion, especially as taught by the Pharisees, Sadducees, lawyers and others.

7. Jesus saw that he might be killed in his desire to inaugurate God's New Age (kingdom). He spoke of this often and especially at the Last Supper (which may have been typical of many meals with his friends.)

8. He was executed as a revolutionary, an enemy of the state, by the Romans, who were aided and abetted by their secular and religious puppets, Herod, the Jewish king and Caiaphas, the Jewish High Priest. They preferred the method of 'nipping in the bud' any possible popular movement. 'Better that one person die, than that the people perish.'

9. The disciples claimed that Jesus had been raised from death, asserting God's approval of him. The Spirit which filled him was now given to them. People today interpret the resurrection of Jesus in many different ways. Some believe that he emerged from his tomb as a recognisable physical person who later rose to heaven. Some believe that he was and is experienced as a spiritual or psychological presence. Others interpret the resurrection stories as a testimony to the continuing endurance of all that Jesus lived for.

Something to think about

What features of the story of Jesus matter most to you?

What do you think of the possibility that the story of Jesus is affected by various authors' own presuppositions and prejudices and by many other people since?

2 Jesus - announcing of Good News

Jesus was known in his own time for bringing good news to people who were excluded from society because they were poor, diseased or handicapped. Many lived on the margins of society; others, often called 'sinners', were for various reasons unable to keep the complex laws of the Jewish faith. Yet others were foreigners ('Gentiles'). He said, 'I came not to call the righteous (i.e. the law-keepers) but sinners'. So who were the poor; who were the 'sinners'?

A) The poor

Note how Luke launches Jesus on his ministry. Jesus takes up the words of Isaiah 61: 'The Spirit of the Lord is upon me because he has anointed me to bring good news to the poor...'. According to Luke, this is the window through which Jesus' life and actions are to be understood. Jesus' beatitudes begin 'Blessed are you poor.' 'Blessed are you hungry.' (Luke 6:20) Clearly the Kingdom is for the poor. Recall John the Baptist's question to Jesus: 'Are you the promised one?' Jesus replied: 'Tell John what you see ... good news is preached to the poor.' (Luke 7:18-23)

Who are the poor?

In the Jewish tradition, the poor are the materially deprived - literally so — including widows, orphans, foreigners: those with no means of support — no land, no territory - they are materially dependent, below the breadline.

In the writings of the Jewish prophets, the poor are also the down-trodden, the oppressed, suffering material poverty and economic and political deprivation. Furthermore, they are helpless and hopeless and can rely only on God. They have nowhere else to go; they recognize their weakness and look to God for help.

The Old Testament has a clear theology of poverty, which Jesus affirms.

There are three strands to this theology:

a) Responsibility for the poor is laid upon the the whole community: e.g. Deuteronomy 15: 7. 'If there is anyone in need, say, a member of your community in any of your towns ... do not be hard-hearted or tight-fisted towards your needy neighbour. You should open your hand, willingly lending enough to meet their need. Be careful you do not entertain a mean thought.... Open your hand to the poor and needy in your land.' This obligation was laid upon the people of God by a solemn 'covenant' or agreement.

Another example:

Deuteronomy 24: 13: If you take a garment as a pledge from a poor man, you must return it the same night, so he can sleep in the cloak.' Also people were instructed to pay wages the same day. Otherwise 'they might cry to the Lord against you and that would incur guilt.'

b) There is Prophetic condemnation of oppression. Isaiah 3: 14: 'The Lord enters into judgement with the elders and princes of his people: It is you who have devoured the vineyard; the spoil of the poor is in your houses. What do you mean by crushing my people, by grinding the face of the poor?' says the Lord. Also see Isaiah 58: 1-10.

c) When God acts, he saves the poor and routs those who oppress them. Many Psalms champion the poor, for example Psalm 12:5. 'Because the poor are despoiled, because the needy groan, I will now rise up, says the Lord. I will place them in safety.' Also Psalm 14:6: 'You shall be put in great terror; you who confound the plans of the poor. For God is their refuge.'

B) Sinners

Mark's gospel begins with proclamation of good news and it is soon very clear that the people for whom the gospel is brought are those called 'sinners' or 'outcasts' : Jesus said, 'I came not to call the righteous, but sinners' : Mark 2: 17.

Jesus was criticized for being with sinners. He is constantly criticised for being with them, eating with them. (Mark 7: 1-13)

Luke's parables of the lost sheep, lost coin and lost son are prompted because he had been criticized for 'welcoming sinners and eating with them.' (Luke 15: 1-2)

Who were these sinners? Psalm 1:1-2 contrasts the 'righteous' with sinners. A sinner is someone who breaks or disregards the law. 'Happy are those who do not follow the advice of the wicked or take the paths that sinners tread... for their delight is in the law of the Lord; and on his law they meditate day and night.'

This is not just a matter of individual morality. It is important to note that the law defines the people corporately. It shows the whole community how they should live as the People of God within a covenant relationship. The Ten Commandments say in effect: 'You are mine; I've saved you so now live like this...'

Keeping the law was not a matter of getting into favour with God; it was a way of living within God's covenant – laws defined boundaries. The sinners were those who did not keep the law and were by definition outside the boundary.

In Ephesians 2:12, Paul sums up the predicament of a sinner as someone who is outside the covenant: 'You were aliens from the commonwealth of Israel and strangers to the covenant of promise, having no hope and without God in the world.'

In Galatians 2:15, Paul refers to Gentiles (non-Jews) being outside the law. In this way Gentiles and sinners alike are regarded as outsiders. Jews too who had abandoned their faith put themselves outside the covenant community. Tax collectors, working for the Romans, are put together with the sinners; they have put themselves outside.

During the Maccabean crisis the Assyrians tried to impose their religion. They tried to suppress loyalty to the Jewish law. So keeping the law became a great mark of being a Jew. Food laws become very important e.g. I Maccabees ch.1. Jews mustn't eat pork. They chose to die rather than profane the covenant.

Until the time of Jesus, keeping the law was a characteristic concern of the Jews. For example, the Pharisees, the 'separated ones' were censorious towards others. People outside their group were beyond the pale. They are not talking about sinners in an absolutist moral sense - immoral, criminal - but in the judgement of those who thought that their understanding of goodness was the only correct one. A very sectarian, fundamentalist attitude was around at the time of Jesus, from those who said: 'We know what God's law requires and we know who is acceptable to God. Only if you agree are you acceptable.'

Jesus saw that it was important to challenge such assumptions. He came to call those regarded as sinners by the righteous. So he shared table company with them. He sought to meet people but was bitterly criticized for befriending sinners: Matt 11:19: 'Look, a glutton and a drunkard, a friend of tax collectors and sinners.'

Note that Jesus is not rushing in to convert sinners. He is not on some kind of evangelistic mission. He is actually affirming them, including them. They have a proper place in God's domain, a notion made clear by his banquet parables (e.g. Luke 14: 12-14): These illustrate the quality of the kingdom; he wants people to live that way. It's a crucial part of middle-eastern culture: to eat with those you wish to be allied with and to receive them into your family.

C) The Embrace of Jesus

Jesus is most critical of the way of exclusion. In the parable of the tax-collector and the Pharisee, the Pharisee reminds God that he has been a good Jew, living as a Jew ought to. 'I'm not like this sinner here'. But Jesus says that the one who is accepted is not the one who counts himself as accepted because he lives in a particular way; rather it's the one who pleads for mercy. Jesus was more critical of those who condemned sinners than he was of the sinners themselves, strikingly so. (Luke 18: 9-14)

Being a sinner has a strong social dimension: it's not just a religious issue. Whole groups are said to be sinners; it's a social description. Jesus was for these people. So if you had asked the poor and the sinners, they would have spoken about a Jesus who brought good news.

If you had asked the rich and the righteous, they would have spoken about a Jesus who brought bad news. It was gospel because once again they were hearing that God is for the alienated, the despised, the outsiders.

Something to consider

Who are 'the poor' in your town and neighbourhood? Do you see any evidence that God is on their side? Who is bringing good news to them?

Whom do you find it hard to include in your circle? Who is excluded by your church, neighbourhood or country? What would be good news for such people?

In what practical ways could you and your community demonstrate "the embrace of Jesus"?

---

3 What did the good news mean for Jesus' disciples?

It meant sharing in the ministry of Jesus – proclaiming good news, identifying with the poor and sinners – a new kind of living. There's a pen sketch of this in the Beatitudes, setting out the character of people who live faithfully in God's realm (Matthew 5: 3-10).

This group of disciples probably had a special internal dynamic. What was character of this new movement?

Here are four features:

A. Jesus – the servant at the centre

Matthew sees Jesus as the new Moses, who calls twelve disciples, reminiscent of the twelve tribes of Israel. It's fascinating that Jesus does not number himself amongst them. He is their leader. See Matthew 23: 8: 'You are not to be called rabbi (teacher), for you have one teacher, and you are all students.' Jesus alone is the teacher. He has authority.

But notice his posture: he chose to serve. So the twelve disciples are not a hierarchy; they are not priests to a laity; Jesus models a new kind of authority:

Mark 9:33-37: The only authority they had was to be like children.

Mark 10: 35-45: Here is a very different model of authority. They must be slaves of others. The one who is ordered around by others is the greatest.

So God's community will engage in a style of ministry which takes its origin from following Jesus. People will reach across social, religious and cultural boundaries; ministry is the antitheses of institutional power with its honorific titles.

B. Circles of discipleship

There's no distinction between those who literally 'left all and followed him' and those he recognized in other ways.

• It's as though his followers were a sequence of circles: the three (Luke 9:28), the twelve (Mark 3:13-18), the seventy-two (Luke 10:1-12).

- There were also fellow travellers, including women. Mary and the other women may have been as close as the twelve (Luke 23:55; 24:8-12).
- Others who stayed at home: Martha and Mary (Luke 10:38-42); Joseph of Aramathea (Luke 23:50-54).
- Jesus had a wide circle of friends. See Mark 3:35 'These are my brothers and sisters - those who do the will of God' – a minimal definition of discipleship, but they are his family.
- The circle goes wider: e.g. Mark 9: the unknown exorcist. He did not follow but Jesus says he is for us - someone who was so obviously doing good.
- Another circle is the poor. (See the Beatitudes: Matthew 5: 3-12)
- A wider circle still are those who feed the hungry, clothe the naked, visit the prisoner - and don't even know Jesus (Matthew 25: 31-46 (especially v. 37-40).

Here is huge diversity; some follow literally; others stay at home. There are all sorts of hidden disciples.

C. Character of openness

There were no boundaries between these circles. They overlapped. There were no outsiders and no insiders. There was no ritual dimension, no baptising. Jesus didn't present any hurdles for people to jump over.

Table fellowship was not just for insiders, it was open to outsiders. This was so offensive to people like the Pharisees, the 'separated ones'. Jesus was touching, eating with and accepting outsiders.

Contrast Jesus' approach to that of the Qumran vision of the assembly of God – a community contemporary to Jesus - depicted in the *Dead Sea Scrolls*.

'No-one who is afflicted with any human impurity may come into the assembly of God; anyone who is afflicted in his flesh; maimed in hand or foot; lame or blind or deaf or dumb; or with a physical mark on his flesh or who is a helpless old man, who cannot stand up in the assembly of the community... These may not enter or take their place in the midst of the community of the men for the holy angels are in their community.

This is a high, austere vision of the community of God in its perfection. No impurity here!

Contrast Jesus' approach:

Look at Luke 14: 21b-22: "Go out at once into the streets and lanes of the town and bring in the poor, the crippled, the blind and the lame.' This is the very antithesis of what the most devout were doing. Whilst they were devoting themselves to keeping the community pure, Jesus was forming a community where purity was banished and impurity welcomed.

So the new community was devoted to breaking down barriers, not least religious barriers. We are not to defend our group and ourselves as though God's grace is limited by our definitions.

D Acceptance and Forgiveness

Discipleship is marked by forgiveness and love. 'Forgive us as we forgive' says the Lord's Prayer (Luke 11: 4). Do we really mean God to take us seriously if we do not forgive? Matthew 18: 21-35 makes it clear that you cannot receive forgiveness if you do not forgive others.

Love of God and love of neighbour go hand in hand; love shows how the law should work out in practice (Luke 10: 25-37).

Something to consider

Jesus' disciples observed his many encounters with all kinds of people:

For whom was he good news?

For whom was he bad news?

4 Who did Jesus become?
Looking at Jesus in the Church

Take a look at the following two paragraphs.

Mark 10:17: "A man ran up, knelt before Jesus and asked him, 'Good Teacher, what must I do to receive eternal life?' 'Why do you call me good?' Jesus asked him, 'No one is good but God alone'." Here Mark depicts Jesus as one who points people to God and away from himself. He is eager to avoid pretentious statements about Jesus.

Nicene Creed: " I believe in one Lord Jesus Christ, the only Son of God, eternally begotten of the Father, God from God, Light from light, true God from true God, begotten not made, one being with the Father." Around 400 years after Mark, the church is eager to describe Jesus as God.

It's clear that there is a world of difference between the Jesus, described in the earliest portrait, Mark, and the Jesus of the creeds and statements of later Christianity.

The distinguished scholar, T.W. Manson, said, way back in 1935,

'We are so accustomed to make Jesus the object of religion, that we are apt to forget that in our earliest records he is portrayed not as the object of religion, but as a religious man'.

Somehow, Jesus, the fervent, charismatic, servant of God - announcer and inaugurator of a New Age - becomes God himself, albeit a co-equal sharer in the life of God: three-in-one, and one-in-three.

Somehow, Jesus, who resisted people's worship, is later worshipped by the church. He, who took the role of a servant, is treated as a conqueror and sovereign.

So what is happening?

In the Gospels, Jesus is portrayed as a charismatic figure, a prophet, a healer, a teacher. He demonstrates an utter commitment to God, whom he called Abba (father). He is a son of God,

But is he God? It is unthinkable that Jesus, a Jew, could have understood himself to be God (see Mark 10: 17-18).

Recently we have begun to appreciate the Jewishness of Jesus.

1. **Jesus respected the Law of Moses,** the foundation of the Jewish way of life. However, he challenged some aspects of the law. Whilst he respected laws which benefitted people and made life better, he was critical of lawyers and priests, who overburdened people with so many rules and regulations. Matthew, especially, sees Jesus as the new Moses, coming with a new Law which embraces all people.

2. **Jesus complied with many of the foundation ideas of the Jewish Law:** He participated in synagogue worship on the Sabbath, visited the Jewish temple as a pilgrim and celebrated the Passover. He committed himself, with his contemporaries, to many of the 'law in a nutshell' sayings of the time, e.g. his twofold summary of the Law: "Love God and your neighbour." Not only Jesus but other sages, like the great Hillel, were said to have uttered, as a summary of the whole Law, sayings like 'Whatever you wish that men do to you, do also to them.'

3. **It is true that Jesus argues against those who insist on the minutiae of the Law,** for example, on Sabbath observance and hand-washing. Throughout Jesus is wanting to emphasise the deeper meaning of these laws, parodying those who get stuck at the level of mere ritual observance. In a sense he is emphasising the spirit of the law. So Jesus in Luke tells us, 'It is easier for heaven and earth to pass away, than for one letter of the Law to fall.' (Luke 16: 17)

4. **Jesus is deeply committed to the inner religious significance of the Law.** He saw the Law as a vehicle for an authentic, living relationship with God the Father, God who is ruler of all.

5. **It seems clear that this is the heart of Jesus' life** - his deep commitment to God. Indeed, Jesus is seen living out this intimate love of God in his relationships with others, especially outcasts and sinners. He treats them as friends. He is imitating what he understands to be the conduct of the Father towards these of his children who are 'afar off' and 'return to him' (Luke 15:11-32).

Jesus is seen as a deeply compassionate Jewish preacher, healer and teacher: committed to the poor and inevitably in conflict with all who oppressed them. This happens because he is overwhelmed by the love and grace of God to everyone. He wants God's people to 'be perfect as their Father in heaven is perfect' (Matthew 5:43-48) not least because God is about to inaugurate his kingdom; there is little time.

BUT very soon, the Jesus movement exploded out of restrictions set by its parent, Judaism. Jesus, proclaimer of a message, became the object of faith, the message itself. This is extraordinary when one considers the temptations Jesus faced himself (Matthew 4: 1-11) and his view of himself, expressed to his friends (Mark 10:35-45; John 13:1-17). Consider how this change might have taken place.

What factors played their part in this transformation?

1. **Church leadership came into the hands of 'Gentiles', non-Jews.** The Gentiles, too, were to be recognized as the 'sons and daughters of the Kingdom', the 'elect of God.'

   In due course, the Torah (the Law of the Jews), which had been the source of Jesus' own spirituality was declared by the church to be not merely optional but null and void. Paul declares, 'Christ is the end of the Law'.

   Also it was in the interests of the Gentile Church to blame the Jews for the death of Jesus; there are whispers of this in the Gospels, especially in John. Blaming the Jews undermined the view that the Christians were enemies of the Roman state. It helped the Christians' case if Jesus was seen to be a victim of Jews, not Romans.

   In the end it was difficult for the Gentile Christians to appreciate their forebears in the Jewish tradition. Jesus, the fervent lover of God, now became the author of truth, the initiator of the message, the beginning and the end. Jesus is substituted for the Jewish Law. Jesus became the new sacrifice - the Lord's Supper replaces the temple and its sacrifices.

2. **The need for permanence when the Kingdom did not come.**

   The life-blood of the mission of Jesus was its eschatological urgency. He believed and taught that the kingdom of God was actually coming into being and would be established in the very near future. This didn't happen.

In due time their eagerness and excitement got transferred to a future return of Christ. That didn't happen either. The resulting emptiness needed to be made good; a corporate body took shape as a quasi-permanent kingdom which was to serve as the repository of religion until the glorious return of Christ one day.

In due course, belonging to the Christian community (the 'brethren' or the 'church'), became central. John's gospel, for example, puts great emphasis upon 'belonging'. A sharp distinction is made between those who are in and those who are outside (John 15:1-6). Sinners are out; loving people are in. If you belong to the truth you are in, if not you are out. This theme runs through the First Epistle of John.

3. **A third factor has to do with a radical shift in part of the central message and role of Jesus.**

   Jesus taught that people were known by God, cherished by God and could access God. The Lord's Prayer sets out an intimate relationship between God and God's people. God provides daily bread; protects people from evil, forgives their sins, longs for people to be forgiving.

   Jesus' deep concern was that people should 'be like their Father in heaven'. 'Be perfect as your Father in heaven is perfect'. But his 'imitation of God' went through a vital change.

   Paul soon began to change this: he wrote to the Ephesians; 'Be imitators of God as beloved children'. So far so good: but he writes later, 'Be imitators of me, as I am of Christ'. **He begins to introduce mediators between God and people:** 'Imitate me, who imitates Christ, who imitates God.'

   Thus originated **a trend in early Christianity to multiply mediators** and intercessors between the faithful and God. It's this business of intermediaries which brings us to the heart of the matter.

Unlike Jesus, **Paul was most pessimistic about human nature.** People are sinful, incapable of obeying God, potentially damned, and lost without the saving grace of Christ's atoning death. Christ's sacrificial blood is needed to cleanse us from sin. Without Christ's redemption, no-one can draw close to God. (Romans 5: 12 – 6:23).

With increasing intensity, the religion of **the early church was focused on the Mediator in place of God.** Prayers continue to be addressed to the Father, but only through the Son.

In due course Jesus disappeared into unapproachable light. As he became judge, the faithful were offered more intermediaries: the apostles, saints and, above all, Mary. Finally, the power of access to God was given to priests, who stole the keys of the kingdom from Peter, standing in the apostolic succession, taking the place of Jesus at the place of sacrifice, the holy table!

Little by little, the Christ of Pauline theology and of the Gentile Church took over from the holy man of Galilee. Jesus's own theocentric devoutness gets overlaid by the ramifications of Paul's christocentric spirituality.

The one who was vindicated by God is enthroned at God's side. He then grows to be the image of God 'The Son is the radiance of God's glory and the exact representation of his being.' (Hebrews 1:3) **Finally he is the equal of God.** So in the early years of the 2nd century, Ignatius Bishop of Antioch writes to Polycarp, Bishop of Smyrna, 'I bid you farewell always in our God, Jesus Christ.'

Such a statement would have been unthinkable in the Palestine of 30 CE, when Jesus walked on to the stage of history. A fervent lover of God, who heralded the Kingdom; indeed who sought to initiate the kingdom; one who was vindicated by God, even raised to life with God, yes: but one who was God? No. That was a notion seized upon by those in another place and time.

4. There is a **fourth** point: **the adoption of the faith by the state,** when Jesus is seen as the one who puts the crown on Constantine's head - the very antithesis of the Temptations. Jesus had to conform or be crucified again. This time he conformed for he was not allowed to speak for himself!

Geza Vermes, one of the greatest scholars to write about the life of Jesus has written:

'And the real Jesus? For there was a real Jesus, without any doubt.

Over the space of months, or perhaps even of two or three years, this real Jesus was seen and heard around the countryside of Galilee and in Jerusalem, an uncompromising, single-minded lover of God and his fellow-beings, convinced that by means of his example and teaching he could infect them with his own passionate sense of relation with the Father in heaven. And he did so. The magnetism of this real Jesus was such that not even the shame and humiliation of the cross, and not even the collapse of his ministry, could extinguish the faith of the men and women of his company. But it is a long time now since he was thought of. Very many ages have passed since the simple Jewish person of the Gospels stepped back and gave way to the rich and majestic figure of the Church's Christ.

Yet it occurs to the historian ... that the world may not have heard the last of the holy Galilean. In this so-called post-Christian era, when Christ as a divine form seems to ever-increasing numbers not to correspond, either to the age's notion of reality, or to the exigencies of the contemporary human predicament, is it not possible that Jesus the healer, teacher and helper may yet be invited to emerge from the shadows of his long exile? And not by Christians alone? If, above all, his lesson on reciprocal, loving and direct relation with the Father in heaven is recalled and found valid, may not the sons and daughters of God on earth stand a better chance of ensuring that the ideal of human sisterhood and brotherhood becomes something more than a pipe-dream?'

(Geza Vermes: The Gospel of Jesus the Jew: Riddell Memorial Lectures 1981: University of Newcastle upon Tyne: ISBN 0 7017 0029 7)

Something to think about:

Recently Philip Pullman wrote a novel, entitled 'The Good Man Jesus and the Scoundrel Christ' (Canongate 2010) in which he exposes the radical difference between the historical Jesus of Nazareth and the Jesus Christ of the Church. In this he draws on the work of many earnest seekers of the Jesus of history.

The Jesus of Mark's Gospel is so different from the Jesus of John's Gospel, let alone the Christ of creed, liturgy and stained glass window.

- *What do you think about this?*
- *Are you able to contemplate the possibility that the Church made Jesus into a person he never was?*
- *If so, is there still value in the living in Way of Jesus?*

5 Jesus and the Way : Jesus and his followers

So far, we've looked at the earliest records of the life of Jesus, seeing how these records drew from memories of Jesus' actions and words. We observed how the early records compared, noting their similarities and differences.

Then we considered **how belief in Jesus developed** over the centuries, especially in the first four centuries. We considered how the followers of Jesus struggled to describe him, after the Christian faith exploded out of its Jewish cradle and attracted believers from the Gentile world, subsequently becoming the official religion first of the Roman Empire and then of Christendom.

This chapter is about **discipleship**, discipleship is about **following**, following is about **Living in the Way.**

It's **not primarily about believing**, for believing is head-stuff and can soon degenerate into being right or wrong. What's the point of having faith, if you don't back it up with the right actions (James 2: 14)?

It's **not only about feelings**, for feelings can be so fickle, so illusory, so variable. The rich young man in Mark's story was so eager, then so gloomy, when Jesus challenged his actions (Mark 10:17-21).

Of course, there are times when we must attend to believing and feeling but just now let's consider **Living** and especially **Living in the Way.**

(Stop and think for a few minutes about 'believing, feeling and living')

So what is the Way?

Well, it's tied up with Jesus. It's what he invited people to, when he said 'Follow me'. The implication was that he was moving off and they were to follow him in the Way.

This notion of 'following in the Way' is particularly strong in Mark.

Read Mark's gospel at a sitting and you get the overwhelming feeling that something new is happening.

- A new age has dawned. People are to shake off the past and grasp the new.

- New things are happening. Jesus is touching the untouchables.
- Evil is being confronted as Jesus challenges anything which binds and oppresses people.
- A new community is being formed. Disciples are being called.

At the centre of it all is Jesus of Nazareth, who appears on the scene right out of the blue. There is no virgin birth, no angelic announcements, no wise men in Mark's gospel. Jesus arrives on the scene, he submits to the baptism of repentance and has to endure all the onslaughts of the devil.

He is called **Son of God,** which is not so much an assertion about his status but of his mission and his relationship with God. Jesus continually asks people not to boast and brag about him. 'Make sure you tell no-one about all this' often comes from his lips. Even when he appears to embrace the idea of Messiahship or divine sonship, he seeks to reinterpret it.

As was said earlier, the strong impression is that the Jesus of the Synoptics would not cope very well with many of the claims made by subsequent generations about him.

So, what are the characteristics of the Way of Living which Jesus advocated and lived out himself?

A task for individuals and groups

Write down some key words which characterise the way of life which Jesus advocated

---

So how did people respond to Jesus?

Looking in **Mark's Gospel**

~ with worship and deference (John the Baptist in Mark 1:7)

~ with belief /recognition (the devils in Mark 1: 24-26)

~ with praise (the people in Mark 1: 27-28)

~ with curiosity (townsfolk in Mark 1: 33,35; 2:2)

~ with argument and debate (scribes in Mark 2:6-8)

~ with astonishment (everyone in Mark 2:12)

None of these is a response which Jesus wants!

Jesus' message is clear, he wants people to follow. And follow they do!

The word *follow* is used

- twice of the crowd,
- six times of the disciples
- four times of the twelve
- nine times of people in general

Following includes many people for varying lengths of time. Those who follow are not as loose a group as the crowd, but they are not as defined a group as the twelve.

Following is not so much a designation of particular people, but rather a word to describe any kind of positive response to the Way which Jesus held out before people (often called the Kingdom of God).

According to Mark, the way to respond to Jesus is not to worship him or stand in awe or to feel guilty, but follow him in the Way. Recall the rebuke of Jesus: 'Why do you call me 'Lord, Lord', when you don't do the things I ask?' (Matthew 7: 15-23).

The next striking impression in the Gospels is **the unlikely assortment of people** who follow Jesus. The trouble is we are so accustomed to the list. Social outcasts (tax collectors & prostitutes), demented people, physically disabled people, those who are immature or feel inferior. He doesn't look for 'whole' people but anyone.

> *Share examples of people, groups, churches who are associating with and even integrating unlikely people into their community.*

The most striking impression in Mark's gospel is that hardly anyone understood what he was about.

The people: followed him for wrong reasons (Mark 1:45, 7:36)
thought he was mad (Mark 3:21)
said he broke the laws (Mark 3:4)

His family: wanted to control him (Mark 3:21)
thought he was a fake (Mark 6:1ff)

Teachers of the Law: he blasphemes (Mark 2:7)
he's demon-filled (Mark 3:22)
he breaks our codes (Mark 7:5)

31

Pharisees: he eats with outcasts (Mark 2:1)

he ignores our fasts (Mark 2:18)

he breaks the Sabbath (Mark 3:4)

But it's the disciples who often come out in a poor light.
This is surprising because we Christians usually pick on all the
others, especially the scribes and Pharisees, but read Mark
through and you'll see that it is the disciples who often didn't
understand:

• The storm on the lake - 'Have you still no faith?' (Mark 4:40)

• Walking on water - 'their minds could not grasp it' (Mark
6:52)

• Discussion about ritual uncleanness - 'don't you understand?'
(Mark 7: 17)

• After the feeding of the 4000 people - 'don't you know or
understand yet?' (Mark 8: 14-21)

Note especially the so-called Caesarea incident, in which
Matthew treats Peter's great statement as a great moment of
insight, whereas Mark and Luke see it as one more example of
the disciples' lack of discernment (Mark 8:27; Matthew 16:13;
Luke 9:18).

Something to think about and discuss:

They didn't understand, but Jesus still invited them to follow.

*If fitness was not a pre-condition of following, what was following
really about?*

*What difference might it make to our church if we really took on
board the idea that following is more important than fitness?*

*What insights can be found in John Bell's hymn: 'Will you come
and follow me?' (on page 39).*

6 Jesus is mine!
Jesus in personal experience

Let's try and understand why we respond in so many different ways to the Jesus-story. By 'the Jesus-story', we mean how Jesus has been depicted, worshipped and followed down the centuries.

Take a look at a variety of paintings of Jesus in books of Christian art, in art galleries, museums and websites. Take a look also at stained glass window depictions in churches. For hundreds of years, artists have depicted Jesus in an enormous variety of ways. Many of them were painted as aids to devotion or to depict the artist's convictions about Jesus. They also served as a focus for particular religious communities, reflecting what was going on in their day.

Download or copy some images of Jesus so that you can spend time looking at them and discussing them with other people.

Then ask yourself what you feel about them. Could you see any of them hanging on your wall at home?

o Which images attract you?

o Which images put you off?

o Which images leave you unmoved?

Why do find some of these pictures attractive?

o Are they what you are accustomed to?

o Do they bring back happy memories / make you feel good?

o Do they express what you believe about Jesus?

Why do you find some of these pictures unattractive ?

o Are they alien to you and your world?

o Are they disturbing / silly / sentimental?

o Do they express the opposite of what you believe about Jesus?

Why do some of these pictures leave you unmoved?

o Do they have nothing to say to you?

o Are they irrelevant?

o Do they belong to a totally different time and place?

If possible, share your reactions with other people.

Pictures are just one way of tapping into experience. Experience has to do with feelings, convictions and ideas - engaging both the right and left sides of the brain!

- The right is about emotion, imagination, feeling, dreaming, colour, texture.
- The left is about thought, logic, reason, analysis, cause and effect.

Some people are guided much more by the left and others by the right. The way we respond may be due to the way we were made as well as by the fund of experience which has influenced us.

Another way of tapping into experience is through hymns and prayers. Think of some hymns which express your experience of Jesus. How about talking to others about your choice? Even sing a few together!

Why do people differ so much in their preferences?

In various ways, **we have been looking at how Jesus has been experienced,** by artists, hymn-writers and story-tellers. We have also looked at how our experience resonates with theirs.

Now to the hard bit! How do we experience Jesus ourselves?

Sit quietly and think of an occasion when the person of Jesus, the words of Jesus or something he did really moved you. Make a note describing where you were, who you were with, etc

Then find someone and tell them briefly about it. Listen to their experience.

We have now heard at least two experiences of Jesus: one of our own and one from someone else. **What do we do with these experiences?**

o How much value do you place on them?

o What do you do if you feel uncomfortable with another person's religious experience?

o How do you check out your own religious experience?

So where do we go from here?

Nothing is free of experience. Whether I am reading, reasoning, singing, fishing, the outcome is always affected by:

o Who I am, with my own particular strengths and needs

o How I am feeling at a particular time

o Who I am with

o Where I am

Indeed it is impossible to be free of all this. This means that there is considerable element of subjectivity in all that we perceive and express. So it is important that our experience is tested in a variety of ways.

Over the years, philosophers and thinkers have reckoned that there are several crucial factors to take into account as we draw conclusions about religious claims:

o **Experience:** how people responded to Jesus, not just individually, but corporately

o **Tradition:** all that has been handed down by the church: scripture, liturgy, etc

o **Reason:** thinking about things and digging deeper

o **Conversation:** checking out together both one's own experience and that of others

So how do we test our experience and that of others? How do we check out our experience of Jesus?

• By talking to other people and hearing what they have got to say, allowing them to probe our ideas and opinions.

• By reading what has been written in hymns and poems, biographies and scholarly research.

• By enjoying religious art, drama and film – maybe retelling the story ourselves.

• Most importantly, by living in Jesus' Way and putting into practice what he said.

In the end, though, we will not be able to speak the last word on any experience, which is why we are left with an extraordinary variety of religious experiences. Indeed we will be left with an extraordinary variety of responses to Jesus. Even in his own life-time, Jesus faced many responses as he called people to follow in the Way.

7 Will you come and follow me?

In previous chapters we looked at the earliest accounts of Jesus' life and ministry. We compared the early records and appreciated their similarities and differences. We have also looked at Jesus' convictions and actions and how people responded to him.

We then considered how belief in Jesus developed over the centuries, especially in the first four centuries. We explored how the followers of Jesus struggled to describe him, once the Christian faith emerged out of its Jewish cradle and attracted believers from the Gentile world and then became the official religion of the Roman Empire and of Christendom.

Finally we looked at Jesus in experience. Using pictures, hymns and personal stories, we saw how varied is the response of people to Jesus. Even in an apparently homogeneous group, one can see how differently people respond - not to mention in different cultures, contexts and times.

So what of our response to Jesus' invitation to follow? Take a look at a crucial passage: Mark 10: 32-52.

The first part of the story contrasts what James and John were looking for and what Jesus was looking for. They wanted to be close to Jesus and they wanted the status which went with it. Jesus said there is no status except that of a slave. This means life-giving service. The disciples couldn't see!

The second part is about the company Jesus kept. The crowds were quite sure that Jesus wanted nothing to do with Bartimaeus. It is interesting that we know his name. Could it be that he became a follower of Jesus? It may well be the case for, at the end of the passage, Mark says that he was able to see and followed Jesus on the road. Which road? The road in verse 32 is the road to Jerusalem and his suffering. Bartimaeus got the point!

Here are some pointers to the kind of response Jesus might just look for if he were here now:

1. There is no status in following, for we are followers, not leaders. Jesus is leader, but see what sort of a leader he is!

2. Jesus is not looking for our worship. He has no desire to be surrounded by sycophants! Could there be too much 'Jesusolatry' in the church? Are there too many hymns and prayers which put Jesus at the centre and which invite people into a love affair with Jesus. Did Jesus want that?

3. Setting our faces towards Jerusalem is tough.

4. The likelihood is that, for the most part, we will only have a partial grasp of what Jesus is about. But the wonder is that he will keep saying 'Follow me'. The amazing thing about the disciples is that they did not understand but he still committed his mission to them.

5. We should not spend too much time trying to get things right by being obsessed with correct theology, biblical interpretation, church order, as if moral, doctrinal or ecclesiological rectitude will improve our discipleship. We'll never be fit!

6. We are likely to be shocked by the company Jesus keeps! Indeed, if we find that we never meet people who have been marginalized, victimised, ignored by society or the church, then it may well be right to assume that, although we have been following somebody, it wasn't Jesus!

7. There's a chance we will suffer with Jesus.

   - Recently a Lancashire Methodist Church, which ran a centre for asylum seekers was firebombed by white racists.
   - A church in West London was burned down twice because they let rooms to a black Pentecostal church.
   - A minister was subjected to hate phone calls because he supported gay people in the life of the church.
   - A boy was bullied by his football team mates because he went to early communion before he played a Sunday morning fixture.
   - A church member was 'sent to Coventry' because he challenged the back-biting which was common currency in his local congregation.

So here's something to think about.

Are you or your church likely to suffer or be misunderstood because you follow where Jesus leads; or are you unlikely to offend anyone?

So what have we discovered so far?

- Jesus invites people to *Follow,* to *live in the Way.*
- The *Way* is tied up with Jesus, his commitment to God, his vision for the world, the choices he made, the challenges he made.
- People responded to him in many ways and still do.
- Jesus doesn't crave people's personal devotion, let alone their worship.
- This *following* will mean walking in difficult places and mixing with uncongenial people.
- You may never finally understand who Jesus was or what motivated him; you will constantly be surprised by his *'Will you ever understand?'*
- There's every chance that, if you get on the road with him, you will suffer with him. It is likely Mark's Gospel was written for catechumens, preparing for baptism at Eastertide. They were to be under no misapprehensions about their calling and commitment. Mark's gospel ends with *'You seek Jesus.* He is risen. *You will not find him here. Go back to Galilee; there you will find him'.* An invitation to recapitulate the journey!

So take yourself off for a while and think through Mark 8: 34 and 35:

'If anyone wants to come after me, they must forget themselves, take up their cross, and follow me. For whoever wants to save his own life will lose it; but whoever loses his life for me and for the gospel will save it.'

Postscript: The Summons

1   Will you come and follow me
        if I but call your name?
    Will you go where you don't know
        and never be the same?
    Will you let my love be shown,
        will you let my name be known,
    will you let my life be grown
        in you and you in me?

2   Will you leave yourself behind
        if I but call your name?
    Will you care for cruel and kind
        and never be the same?
    Will you risk the hostile stare
        should your life attract or scare?
    Will you let me answer prayer
        in you and you in me?

3   Will you let the blinded see
        if I but call your name?
    Will you set the prisoners free
        and never be the same?
    Will you kiss the leper clean,
        and do such as this unseen,
    and admit to what I mean
        in you and you in me?

4   Will you love the 'you' you hide
        if I but call your name?
    Will you quell the fear inside
        and never be the same?
    Will you use the faith you've found
        to reshape the world around,
    through my sight and touch and sound
        in you and you in me?

5   Lord, your summons echoes true
        when you but call my name.
    Let me turn and follow you
        and never be the same.
    In your company I'll go
        where your love and footsteps show.
    Thus I'll move and live and grow
        in you and you in me.

Suggestions for Further Reading

John Bell,
10 Things they never told me about Jesus (2009)

Marcus J. Borg,
Jesus: Uncovering the Life, Teachings, and Relevance of a Religious Revolutionary (2008)

Marcus J. Borg,
Meeting Jesus Again for the First Time (1995)

David Boulton,
Who on Earth was Jesus? (2008)

John Dominic Crossan,
Jesus: A Revolutionary Biography (1995)

John Dominic Crossan,
The Greatest Prayer (2011)

Robert Funk,
A Credible Jesus (2002)

Roy Hoover,
Profiles of Jesus (2002)

Neil MacGregor,
Seeing Salvation: Images of Christ in Art (2002)

Methodist Church,
Collection of Modern Christian Art
www.methodist.org.uk/static/artcollection

Mark Allan Powell,
The Jesus Debate (1998)

John Shelby Spong,
Jesus for the Non-Religious (2007)

Geza Vermes,
Searching for the Real Jesus: Jesus, the Dead Sea Scrolls and other Religious Themes (2010)

Wild Goose Publications:
Various resource material on Jesus.
See the website www.ionabooks.com